Date Due

Roller Coasters

Gil Chandler

Illustrated with photographs
by Tom Maglione and Paul L. Ruben

Reading consultant:

John Manning, Professor of Reading
University of Minnesota

Capstone Press

MINNEAPOLIS

C A P S T O N E   P R E S S

2440 Fernbrook Lane • Minneapolis, Minnesota 55447

Printed in the United States of America.

Library of Congress Cataloging-in-Publication Data
Chandler, Gil, 1958-
   Roller coasters / by Gil Chandler.
   p. cm.
   Includes bibliographical references and index.
   ISBN 1-56065-221-7
   1. Roller coasters--Juvenile literature. [1. Roller coasters.] I. Title.
GV1860.R64C42 1995
791'.06'8--dc20

                        94-30621
                          CIP
                          AC

The publisher acknowledges the generous help of the American Coaster Enthusiasts, especially Randy Geisler, Ray Ueberroth, Tom Maglione and Nancy Stillwagon.

Table of Contents

Chapter 1
The First Drop

You climb into the little car. The operator places an iron bar across your lap and locks it into place. You can't stand up, move around, or get out.

The car begins to climb a long, tall hill of wooden beams. You're moving up the hill, tilted back, facing the sky. Underneath, a clanking chain pulls the car upward. The people on the ground are getting smaller and smaller.

The car slows at the top of the hill. The clanking sound ends as you hang in space. You try not to look down. It's ten stories to the trees and buildings and pavement below.

The car jerks forward and rushes toward the ground. At the last second, it pulls up. There's a curve, a drop, a bump, and another bump. People are screaming. Some are raising their arms. Most are just hanging on.

You hold tight to the lap bar. Your stomach leaps and dives with the coaster. The **g-forces** make you feel light as the coaster rises and heavy as it dips. Around the curves, your body slams to the right and then to the left.

A little more than sixty seconds has gone by. The hills get smaller and smaller. Then you go into a black tunnel. At the end of the tunnel the car sinks away beneath you again. A turn, a rise, and a spiraling dip take your breath away. Finally, the car slows into the last turn. The track levels out.

Your head spins and you're breathing hard. It's time to go–but you can hardly stand up.

Right, the Kennywood *Thunderbolt.*

Chapter 2

"Steelies" and "Woodies"

There are two kinds of roller coasters: wood coasters ("woodies") and steel coasters ("steelies"). Wooden coasters ride on metal rails supported by wooden boards, like a set of train tracks. The hills and curves rest on a huge frame of wooden beams. This is the oldest kind of roller coaster.

Steel coasters, which run over a long steel tube, began to appear in the 1960s. The use of steel completely changed roller coasters. They can carry coaster cars through upside-down **loops**, **corkscrews**, and steeply banked turns. Steel also allows designers to build coasters that hang from an overhead track.

Many people prefer the old-fashioned wooden coasters–the "woodies." They enjoy the creaking of the wooden frame and the clickety-clack of the car wheels running over the tracks. They enjoy a steep drop and a vicious curve.

There are more than 200 roller coasters operating in North America. Here are some of the most famous rides. Some are steel, some are wood. Which is better? Read about them. Try them out. Decide for yourself.

The Cyclone
Astroland, Coney Island, Brooklyn, New York

This is the granddad of all modern roller coasters. *The Cyclone's* cars took their very first drop in 1927.

There is an odd squeaking and creaking as you ride up *The Cyclone's* first hill. Don't worry, the builders designed it that way! Wooden beams that move will last longer than rigid ones. They bend a little with the weight of the cars–and they squeak.

From the top, you drop 85 feet (26 meters) at an angle of 60 degrees–the steepest drop of any coaster. Then you cruise at 50 miles (80 kilometers) per hour. Eight hills lift you up and slam you back down in your seat. Sharp curves push you back and forth in the car as you hang on for your life.

After it opened, *The Cyclone* was an instant hit. Roller-coaster designers copied the design all over the country. They never quite matched the thrill of the original Coney Island *Cyclone*.

Steel Phantom

Kennywood Park, West Mifflin, Pennsylvania

The *Steel Phantom* reaches a speed of 80 miles (129 kilometers) per hour–the fastest coaster, of any kind, on earth. The first hill on the *Phantom* twists and turns through a drop of 157 feet (48 meters). The second hill runs 225 feet (69 meters) through a narrow gorge and over and under the tracks of another coaster. This is the longest drop ever built. Before the

Bobsled coasters follow a smooth, rounded steel chute.

ride is over, passengers also zip through a loop, a **boomerang**, a corkscrew, and a **helix**.

Avalanche
Kings Dominion, Doswell, Virginia

Riders have to hold on tight on this **bobsled** ride, which follows a smooth, rounded steel chute instead of a track. Instead of small train

cars, the *Avalanche* features metal cars that look like bobsleds.

The first drop is a long, downward spiral. At the end, the eight-car trains turn through a complete circle, first upward and then downward.

Run-A–Way Mine Train
Six Flags Over Texas, Arlington, Texas

This 2,400-foot (732-meter) steel ride is a modern version of the very first American coaster, the *Mauch Chunk Switchback Railway*, in Mauch Chunk, Pennsylvania. It was the first modern **mine train**. As the ride drops, turns, and dips, you feel as if you're riding on a

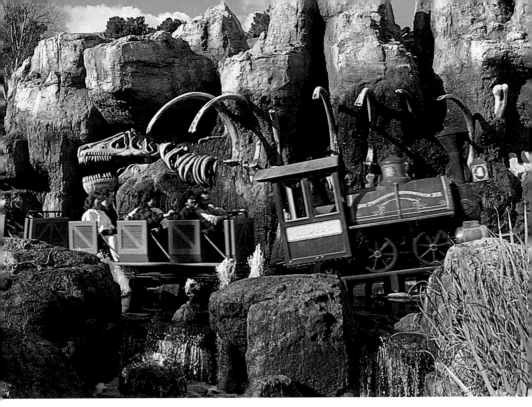

Big Thunder Mountain Railway at **Disneyworld**

runaway train. The cars also pass through a
hotel and a saloon!

The Beast
Kings Island Park, Kings Mill, Ohio

The Beast is 7,400 feet (2,256 meters) long–
the world's longest wooden coaster. There are
two steep lift hills and two long tunnels. The
ride cuts a long, fast, curving path through a

nearby forest and along the side of a hill. Riders take the final stretch at 60 miles (97 kilometers) per hour through a tunneled helix.

Loch Ness Monster
Busch Gardens, Williamsburg, Virginia

The *Monster's* first drop leaves you dangling just above the surface of a river. Soon you're flying around the steel track at 60 miles (97 kilometers) per hour. At the end of two full loops, another car is coming straight at you. The car is timed so that it rolls away into an upside-down loop of its own at the last second. Whew!

Twister (formerly Mr. Twister)
Elitch Gardens, Denver, Colorado

This amazing wooden coaster is 3,020 feet (920 meters) long and 96 feet (29 meters) high. It was redesigned in 1965, when wooden coasters were coming back in style.

Steel roller coasters, such as the *Loch Ness Monster*, can take loops and curves that would be impossible on a woodie.

Twister does everything a "woodie" can possibly do, including a brief stretch of **air time**. The ride also includes a **double helix** and a speeding run through a dark tunnel.

King Cobra
Kings Island Park, Kings Mill, Ohio

An arm harness and a lap bar hold you in place. You'll need them both. You're standing up! *King Cobra* was the first stand-up coaster built in the United States.

Your entire body, and especially your legs, will really feel the g-forces as the "Snake" speeds through a loop, a vicious spiral turn, and a series of **camelbacks**. It's just like flying through the air.

Le Monstre
La Ronde Amusement Park, Montreal, Quebec

Two coaster trains ride at the same time around this exciting double-track coaster. Twelve times during the run, the trains pass each other in a **crisscross**. The riders also get

a surprise as the cars hop and dip through spectacular, scary turns.

Big Bad Wolf
Busch Gardens, Williamsburg, Virginia

When you first climb into the *Big Bad Wolf*, you notice something funny about the car. It's not riding on any tracks. It's attached to an overhead track!

Big Bad Wolf was the first **suspended coaster**. The cars swing out from the steel track–to the right, to the left, and back again. They rise, fall, and turn along steep hills and through a forest. Right behind you is a growling wolf, chasing you down a steep ravine and over the top of a village. At the end, the cars squeeze past jets of water at almost 50 miles (80 kilometers) per hour and make a steep drop to a calm, clear river. This is one ride that really leaves you hanging!

Big Bad Wolf **takes riders on a thrilling chase–suspended in the air!**

Chapter 3
Rolling in a Coaster

All coasters run on the same fuel–**gravity**. Gravity is the force that attracts a small object towards a larger one. The largest object in our world is the earth itself. Gravity pulls people, buildings, trees, and roller coasters downwards, toward the center of the earth.

G-force
One measure of gravity is called a g-force. When you are standing still, gravity pulls on you with a force of 1 g-force, or 1 g. And when you are moving, the force of **inertia** keeps you moving. Inertia resists any change in speed or direction.

How Many G's?

At the start of the ride, a chain attached to a motor drags the train up the tallest hill. As the coaster rises, it stores up **potential energy**. At the top, the chain lets go of the cars. This is the famous first drop that all coasters have. On the first drop, the force of gravity converts the potential energy into **kinetic energy**.

Up and Down, Back and Forth

When the coaster rolls down a high, steep track, the cars gradually **accelerate**. The higher the track, the faster the acceleration. Faster and faster, the cars and your body are moving back down towards the surface of the earth.

When the coaster suddenly turns upward again, you feel the effects of inertia–the force that resists the change in direction. Inertia increases the g-forces on your body, pressing you down in your seat. You actually weigh more.

But when you're racing upward to the top of the hill, inertia again takes effect. It is pushing the cars–and you–upward. This decreases the g-forces when the coaster turns back down the

hill. You feel negative g's, and you weigh less than you normally do. If you weren't strapped in, you might float right out of your seat.

One other kind of force is at work during a roller coaster ride. **Centrifugal** force pushes things that are moving in a circle outward, away from the center of the circle. It affects you when the cars turn around a curve or go upside down in a loop. If the coaster turns sharply to the left, centrifugal force pushes you outwards, to the right. If a coaster turns right, your body moves to the left.

As the coaster rolls back into the station, all the potential energy that built up on the lift hill is gone. The kinetic energy reaches zero. As motion slows, inertia no longer has any effect, and the g-forces return to 1. Your weight returns to normal, and the coaster comes to a smooth stop.

When you ride a roller coaster, you are feeling all these forces–potential energy, kinetic energy, gravity, inertia, and centrifugal force–work on your body.

Chapter 4

Coaster History

The Russians built the very first **gravity rides** in the 1600s. In winter, they built high wooden ramps and covered them with water, which soon became ice. The ramps were about two feet (.6 meter) wide–just wide enough for a small sled.

Passengers would climb a 70-foot (21-meter) ladder, then sit down on the sled. A helper pushed the sled onto the ramp. Down it went, speeding to the bottom of the hill and then coasting to a stop along a 600-foot (183-meter) straightaway.

People in big cities and small villages enjoyed the ice slides. They were built outside

Right, an early Russian ice slide

in public parks and even inside in fancy palaces. Some of the ramps had lanterns for night sliding.

In the early 1800s, a French builder brought the "Russian mountains" to Paris, the capital of France. But Russia was much colder than France, where ice turned soft in the warmer, rainy winters. So the French ran their sleds over wooden rollers. This is the origin of the term "roller coaster."

Coasters Cross the Atlantic

In the 1870s, an old mining railway became the first gravity ride in the United States. This was the *Mauch Chunk Switchback Railway* in Pennsylvania. A steam engine hauled the cars up a mountain. The cars then coasted down at six miles (10 kilometers) per hour. Passengers on the *Mauch Chunk Railway* paid five cents a ride.

In 1884, LaMarcus A. Thompson designed a new coaster for Coney Island, an amusement park in Brooklyn, New York. Thompson's *Switchback Gravity Pleasure Railway* was a big hit. Thompson built 44 more of these rides in North America and Europe.

Other coaster inventors like Phillip Hinckle and Lina Beecher began working at Coney Island. Hinckle was the first to use a chain lift to get his cars up the hill. Beecher built the *Flip-Flap,* the first coaster to run upside-down through a loop. The cars had to go so fast to make it through the loop, however, that several riders suffered **whiplash**. The *Flip-Flap* soon shut down.

By the 20th century, roller coasters had much more than single cars and simple ramps. The builders put tracks through turns, hills, and figure-eights. The inventor John Miller added a third set of wheels, known as undertrack wheels. The undertrack wheels held the cars firmly on the track at high speeds and through sharp turns.

The Golden Age

Roller coasters were all the rage in the 1920s. Designers were making them taller, longer, and faster. Some lift hills climbed as

LaMarcus A. Thompson.

high as 100 feet (30 meters). The Coney Island *Cyclone*, built in 1927, rose 85 feet (26 meters) and ran at 55 miles (89 kilometers) per hour over eight steep hills.

The Depression of the 1930s and World War II (1939-1945) put an end to this **Golden Age of Roller Coasters**. Fewer people were going to amusement parks. There was a shortage of the money and materials needed to build new rides. Instead of raising new coasters, workers were tearing down hundreds of them.

Disneyland

In 1955, Walt Disney reversed this trend. He built a new amusement park in Anaheim, California. This was the first **theme park**, Disneyland.

In 1959, the *Matterhorn* opened at Disneyland. This was a steel roller coaster that turned and twisted down the sides of a miniature steel-and-concrete mountain. At the end of the ride, the cars–four-passenger bobsleds–splashed through a pool of water. It became one of the most popular rides in Disneyland.

Other theme parks appeared around the country. Each had a new roller coaster. At Six Flags Over Mid-America, in Eureka, Missouri, the *Screamin' Eagle* rose 110 feet (34 meters). In 1975, it was the highest wooden coaster in the world.

The Age of Steel Roller Coasters

Wooden coasters were expensive to build. And wood limited the shape of the ride and what the cars could do. So coaster designers in the late 1960s turned to steel. Long steel tubes could twist and turn in all directions. This allowed coaster designers to create new thrills for their riders. The age of steel roller coasters had begun.

Chapter 5
Building a Roller Coaster

From the earliest days, coaster designers have tried to make the rides better and better. To design the Coney Island *Cyclone*, builders used pencil and paper to plan their hills, curves, and dips. This was good enough for the classic wood coasters. Nowadays, it takes a team of skilled engineers and architects to create the looping, twisting, and corkscrewing steel coasters.

Building *Kumba*

Kumba is a steel coaster that opened at Busch Gardens in Tampa, Florida, in 1993. It took four years to design and build *Kumba*.

Bolliger and Mabillard, a Swiss company, used a computer to figure out how much kinetic energy the ride would build up on the first lift. The computer also showed how long the cars would run before losing their potential energy. Designers knew the g-forces and the speed of the cars at every point along the ride.

The company prepared 500 sets of **blueprints** to design *Kumba*. Three-dimensional models made out of Styrofoam and balsa wood were built. The track would include 124 sections of steel tube, each of them 30 feet (10 meters) long. Each section had to fit perfectly with the next.

A factory manufactured the track sections, then sent them to the building site. Workers poured concrete bases, called **footings**, to support the columns that would hold up the track. After the columns were in place, they laid each section of the track into position.

The building of *Kumba* turned out to be a great success. The track sections fit together perfectly. Not once did the workers need to pound or force the sections into place.

Test Dummies in Coasters

After the lift motor for the first hill was in place, the cars were installed. Then the roller coaster went through dozens of test runs. Sometimes the cars were empty, sometimes they carried sandbags or **mannequins**. Finally, the workers who designed and built the track rode the coaster.

When the test runs were over, it was time to open the ride to eager, paying customers. The many years of work and worry began to pay off.

Strong concrete footings support the weight of the tracks.

Chapter 6
Rolling Into the Future

Roller coasters are changing all the time. Coaster builders are always coming up with new designs and new thrills for their riders. The future promises higher, longer tracks, and higher speeds. And some amazing new effects may become an ordinary part of the roller coaster of the future.

Some of the new coasters won't really roll at all. Instead, their passengers will sit on a large platform that sways, rises, and dips beneath them. A screen that surrounds them will display exciting scenes–a thundering volcano, a convoy of jets in formation, or a trip into outer space. The moving platform makes the riders feel that they're really in the scene.

Other rides will use a technology called **virtual reality**. In a virtual-reality ride, you will sit on the platform while wearing a helmet that covers your eyes. A computer will project an exciting ride onto a viewing screen in your helmet.

The first virtual-reality theme park has already been built. In the summer of 1994, a computer-game company named Sega Enterprises opened Joyopolis near Tokyo, Japan. Other virtual-reality parks may soon open in North America.

Le Monstre at **La Ronde.**

Glossary

accelerate–to increase speed

air time–the feeling due to negative g's

blueprints–plans for building something, showing all shapes and measurements

bobsled–a ride that runs over a smooth track of wood or steel instead of rails

boomerang–a ride that runs back and forth over the same track, going through loops and over hills

camelback hills–a series of small hills that look like the humps of a camel

centrifugal force–the force that pushes outward on an object turning in a circle or around a curve

corkscrew turn–a series of loops that are stretched out in a long spiral

crisscross–a point at which the tracks of one coaster ride cross the tracks of another

double helix–two turns which change elevation constantly

footings–concrete bases buried deeply in the ground

g-force–a measure of the pull of gravity on an object or person. One g-force is equal to the force of earth's gravity, at sea level, on an object that is not moving.

Golden Age of Roller Coasters–a period during the 1920s when roller coasters were most common

gravity ride–any ride that uses gravity for power

helix–a turn that changes elevation constantly

inertia–the force that resists any change in the speed or direction of an object

kinetic energy–energy due to the speed of a moving object

loop–a complete circle

mannequins–human-shaped forms made of wood or plastic

mine train–a coaster ride that looks and feels like a runaway mine car

potential energy–energy that is stored as a roller coaster moves uphill

suspended coaster–a ride that hangs from an overhead rail

theme park–an amusement park built around an idea, such as a historical event or entertainment personality

virtual reality–a technology in which a computer sends three-dimensional pictures to a helmet worn by a viewer

whiplash–a severe sprain of the neck caused by sudden movement or twisting of the head

To Learn More

Ambrosini, Allen and Randy Geisler, editors. *Guide to Ride: A Guide to the Roller Coasters of North America.* Chicago: American Coaster Enthusiasts, 1991.

Silverstein, Herma. *Scream Machines.* New York: Walker and Company, 1986.

Van Steenwyk, Elizabeth. *Behind the Scenes at the Amusement Park.* Niles, IL: Albert Whitman, 1983.

Weise, Jim. *Roller Coaster Science.* New York: Wiley, 1994.

Some Useful Addresses

American Coaster Enthusiasts (ACE)
Box 8226
Chicago, IL 60680

National Amusement Park Historical Association
P.O. Box 83
Mt. Prospect, IL 60056

Index